DEFENCE OF THE NATIONAL DEMOCRACY AGAINST THE ATTACK OF JUDGE DOUGLAS—CONSTITUTIONAL RIGHTS OF THE STATES.

SPEECH

OF

HON. J. P. BENJAMIN,

OF LOUISIANA.

DELIVERED IN THE SENATE OF THE UNITED STATES, MAY 22, 1860.

Mr. PRESIDENT: When we met here in December the public mind was deeply stirred. It was stirred by an occurrence which had taken place for the first time in our history—the invasion of one of the States of the Confederacy by a band of fanatics for the avowed purpose of interfering with its domestic institutions and setting its slaves at liberty. The whole country was deeply stirred, but especially stirred was the South, and this universal excitement found immediate vent in Congress. Scarcely had we met, when numerous resolutions were placed upon our table by different Senators, which, on the 2d of February, were ordered, by a resolution of the Senate, to be printed together. The first was a resolution submitted by the honorable Senator from Ohio, (Mr. PUGH,) who, on the 15th of December, proposed that the Committee on Territories

"Be instructed to inquire into the expediency of repealing so much of the acts approved September 9, 1850, for the organization of territorial governments in New Mexico and Utah, as require that all the laws passed by the legislatures of those Territories shall be submitted to Congress for approval or rejection."

That was offered on the 15th of December, before even the House of Representatives had been organized. To that an amendment was offered by the Senator from Iowa, (Mr. HARLAN,) which I shall not read. The next was a resolution submitted on the 16th of January by the Senator from Illinois, (Mr. DOUGLAS,) in relation to instructions to the Committee on the Judiciary to report a bill for the protection of the States and Territories of the Union against invasion. Next, on the 18th of January, were resolutions submitted by the Senator from Mississippi, (Mr. BROWN.) Next, were amendments to those resolutions submitted by the Senator from Minnesota, (Mr. WILKINSON.) Next, were the resolutions submitted by the other Senator from Mississippi, (Mr. DAVIS,) on the 2d of February; and, finally, to those resolutions amendments were offered by the Senator from Delaware, (Mr. SAULSBURY.)

Here, then, was a series of propositions before the Senate, seven in number, all directed to the question of slavery in the States and Territories, and all ordered by the Senate "to be printed together for discussion." Under these circumstances, it became obvious that, unless some concert of action was had by gentlemen who professed the same political principles in relation to this vital issue now before the country, the discussion must be confused and pointless. If every member offered his own resolutions in his own language, and if there was no concert among those who entertained the same principles, the time of the Senate would be needlessly exhausted, and we should come to no practical result. Under these circumstances, a suggestion was made, from what quarter I know not, and certainly it is not of the slightest consequence, that the members of the Democratic party, who were supposed generally to entertain sentiments in accordance with each other, should meet and should agree upon the phraseology of the resolutions that they were disposed to support, and,

Printed by Lemuel Towers, at $1 50 per hundred copies.

after harmonizing upon that phraseology, should agree to stand by it, with a view to get a vote of the Senate upon distinct propositions, as the principles of the Democratic party, so far as that party was represented by the Senators in Congress.

Now, Mr. President, these resolutions being before us, the honorable Senator from Illinois, (Mr. DOUGLAS,) the other day—I am sorry that I do not see him in his seat; I should have waited for him, if I had the slightest hope of seeing him in the Senate; he was not here yesterday; he is not here to-day; and it is impossible for any one of us to say when he will be here again—the honorable Senator from Illinois, in one of the most extraordinary speeches ever delivered in a deliberative body, and which occupies over twenty consecutive columns of the Globe, and which was followed, a day or two after, in reply to the Senator from Mississippi, (Mr. DAVIS,) by several other columns, has undertaken what certainly is without precedent in the history of the country—has undertaken to defend his individual claims to the Presidency of the United States; and, in so doing, has divided out his elaborately-prepared speech into different portions, some of which alone shall I attempt to answer; and I attempt that answer because that Senator thought proper to arraign my State and to arraign me, with other Democratic States and other Democratic Senators, for daring to discuss the propositions and resolutions now before the Senate.

More than half of that Senator's speech was devoted to the perfectly idle and unnecessary task of proving that those principles which he now asserts to be the true constitutional principles under which the Territories of the United States are governed, were advocated by him as such years and years ago; and therefore he undertook to prove to the Senate and to the country—to which he appealed so often—that there has been no inconsistency in his course, and that if he and his brother Democratic Senators are at issue upon any point, it is we, and not he, who have proved inconsistent. I shall return to that, sir, in a moment.

The next proposition of the honorable Senator from Illinois was, that he was the embodiment of the Democratic party, and that all who dissented from this modest proposition were rebels. He next arraigned all his Democratic brethren in this Chamber for daring to offer resolutions to the Senate declaratory of constitutional principles; and he called the resolutions now before us a caucus platform, which he said the Charleston convention, which represents him, treated with the scorn and contempt that they merited.

Next he said that seventeen Democratic States of this Union, and all his brother Democratic Senators who did not agree with him, were disunionists, and he arraigned them as such. He said that they were traveling on the high road to the disunion of these States. Then, in the plenitude of his indulgence, he told us that we were sinning through ignorance and did not know what road we were traveling, and, with princely magnanimity, tendered his clemency and his pardon to those who, after being enlightened by his counsel, should tender repentance. And after having done all that—having attacked every Democratic State in the Union, and almost every Democratic Senator in this body, he closed with a statement that all that he had said was in self-defence; that he attacked nobody, and that the world should know, if he ever spoke again, it would be, as he had just then spoken, to defend himself from attack.

Now, Mr. President, lest I should be supposed to have at all exaggerated, in this statement, what the honorable Senator from Illinois thought proper to say in relation to resolutions involving purely constitutional and political principles, I will read here and there passages from his speech, in support of the assertion that I made. In relation to the action of his brother Senators, he says this:

"Sir, let the Democratic Senators attend to their official duties, and leave the national conventions to make their platforms, and the party will be united. Where does this trouble come from? From our own caucus chambers—a caucus of Senators dictating to the people what sort of platform they shall have. You have been told that no less than twelve southern Senators warned you in the caucus against the consequences of trying to force senatorial caucus platforms on the party. Sir, I do not know when the people ever put it in a Senator's commission that he is to get up platforms for the national conventions, on the supposition that the delegates who go there have not sense enough to do it themselves.

"Although the action of the caucus was heralded to the world to be, as was generally understood, for the purpose of operating on the Charleston convention, it did not have its effect.

The resolutions lay still. When it was proposed to postpone them here in the Senate, before the Charleston convention, I voted against the postponement. I wanted to give a chance for a vote on them before the party acted. I did not believe the party then would agree to the dictation. I do not think they would obey the order. Sir, the Charleston convention scorned it, and ratified the old platform."

I appeal to the Senate whether or not this is self-defence. I appeal to the Senate whether or not this be, as I have stated it to be, an arraignment by the honorable Senator from Illinois against the action of almost the entire body of his brother Democrats—a perversion of the truth and the facts, a misrepresentation of what occured; for this, namely, that the meeting of the Senators who adopted a series of resolutions, which they believed to be sound constitutional doctrine, was based upon the fact that a large series of independent resolutions had been put before the Senate, and that some concerted action of the party in relation to those resolutions was just as necessary as the concerted action of the parties who supported the Kansas-Nebraska bill in 1854, when the honorable Senator from Illinois called them into council every morning almost of his life during that controversy. When that bill was pending; when amendments were offered around the Chamber, for the purpose of concentrating action and preventing that division of the party which might be taken advantage of by the opponents upon the floor of the Senate, the honorable Senator from Illinois called together those who supported the bill every morning, and asked their opinions, and changed and modified the phraseology to suit all and to obtain the assent of all. That was the purpose of the Democratic Senators who met to consider resolutions that Senators all around the Chamber had offered. That they did; and that is what has been perverted into an attempt to dictate a party platform to a convention.

Nay, more, sir, in order that there might be no possibility of misrepresenting those resolutions as being the dictation of a party platform, the Senate postponed the consideration of the resolutions until after the party had met and made what the Senator from Illinois says is its platform; and that very postponement is brought up here as an arraignment of the intentions of the Senators, who are now speaking on these resolutions after the platform has been made, as he says. It was with the view, as he now says, to affect his presidential chances. I leave that accusation for what it is worth. I have stated the accusation, and stated the defence.

Next, sir, I say that the honorable Senator from Illinois, not satisfied with discussing the constitutional questions now before the Senate upon their merits, has thought proper to arraign seventeen Democratic States of this Union as disunionists. He accompanies it with the suggestion that he forgives us, because we know not what we do. I say, sir, the fact that the Senator from Illinois arraigns seventeen Democratic States, and nearly all his Democratic brethren here, as disunionists, I will also show, by an extract from his speech the other day, of a few lines. He tells us that these resolutions are a Yancey platform; and that the resolutions reported to the Charleston convention by a majority of the States of this Union, by the almost unanimous assent of the Democratic States of the Union, was a Yancey platform also; and that Yancey made the platform for the party, made the caucus platform, and made the platform for the majority of the Democratic States of the Union; and that all, together with Yancey, we are disunionists. Here is his language, sir:

"The Yancey platform at Charleston, known as the majority report from the committee on resolutions, in substance and spirit and legal effect, was the same as the Senate caucus resolutions; the same as the resolutions now under discussion, and upon which the Senate is called upon to vote.

"I do not suppose that any gentleman advocating this platform in the Senate means or desires disunion. I acquit each and every man of such a purpose; but I believe, in my conscience, that such a platform of principles, insisted upon, will lead directly and inevitably to a dissolution of the Union. This platform demands congressional intervention for slavery in the Territories in certain events. What are these events? In the event that the people of a Territory do not want slavery, and will not provide by law for its introduction and protection, and that fact shall be ascertained judicially, then Congress is to pledge itself to pass laws to force the Territories to have it."

So, sir, these resolutions are a "Yancey platform," a caucus platform, a disunion platform; and the purpose is, of all who support them and vote for them, after the people of a Territory shall have decided that "they do not want slavery, and that fact has been ascertained judicially, to get Congress to force slavery on them." That is the deliberate statement, prepared and put forth to the world, revised and corrected by the honorable Senator from Illinois. Mr. President, my State voted for that platform. I shall vote for this caucus-Yancey platform, if that helps the Senator from Illinois. If it helps him to give nicknames, and he thinks that an appeal to the people of the country will be helped by accusing Democratic States and Democratic Senators of being led by a gentleman whom he supposes to be unpopular, and calls them supporters of a Yancey platform and of a disunion platform, let him have the benefit of such appeal. I, for my part, accept the responsibility, and stand by the resolutions and the platform. But, sir, at the same time I deny that there is the slightest approach to truth or correctness in the lineaments ascribed by the honorable Senator from Illinois to the platform adopted by the majority of the Democratic States at Charleston, or to the principles which are here advocated by the almost unanimous vote of the Democratic Senators. I deny that there is the least approach to truth in his picture. No man here has called upon Congress to force slavery upon an unwilling people. No man here has called upon Congress to intervene and force slavery into the Territories. No man has asked Congress to do what the gentleman speaks of in another part of his speech as making a slave code for the Territories—that being another of the slang phrases which the honorable Senator from Illinois adopts from Republican gentlemen at the North, and parades to the American people as proof that he is sound on this subject of the Democracy, and that we are unsound. No man has asked for such a thing, or anything approaching to such a thing, as I shall proceed hereafter to show

Now, Mr. President, having shown to you the charges made by the honorable Senator from Illinois against the Democratic States of this Confederacy, and the Democratic Senators in this Hall—which charges I repel and mean to disprove to-day—I desire to read a few words which I find at the close of his speech, for the purpose of showing how nearly and how closely his conclusions and his speech accord with what I have just stated:

"I am sorry to have been forced to occupy so much of the time of the Senate; but the Senate will bear me witness that I have not spoken, in the last two years, on any one of these topics, except when assailed, and then in self-defence. You will never find the discussion renewed here again by me, except in self-defence. I have studiously avoided attacking any man, because I did not mean to give a pretext for renewing the assault on me; and the world shall understand that if my name is brought into this debate again, it will be done aggressively, as an assault on me; and if I occupy any more time, it will be only in self-defence."

Mr. President, this mode of discussing public subjects is a very convenient one—arraigning every gentleman sitting here on this side of the Chamber, attacking them in the most offensive of all manners; spreading that attack, revised and corrected, in the official columns of the Globe, issuing it out to the world; and then saying that if any man should raise his voice here to repel it, it will be an assault on him, and the world shall know that he does not speak except in self-defence. He makes it impossible to answer his charges without attacking his course, and then says he is driven by self-defence to fresh assaults! I am afraid, Mr. President, that I shall be obnoxious to the charge of assailing the honorable Senator from Illinois, if it be indeed an assault to repel a most wanton and unprovoked attack.

More than one-half the speech of the honorable Senator from Illinois was devoted, as I said before, to the purpose of proving his own consistency, from some period which I do not care to go back to, down to 1854 and 1856, and the present time. He says he is now consistent with the principles that he then professed. I do not deny it. I do not know that anybody denies it. On the contrary, that is the precise charge brought against him, as I shall proceed to show. The precise charge is that, having agreed with us that he would abandon those principles, if they were proved to be false, he now flies from his bargain; he now denies what he agreed to; he now refuses to be bound by that to which he had previously given his consent; and defends himself, because, as he says, he is now in accordance with what he was then. I do not propose to go back beyond the year 1857; because every one here knows that, up to the year 1857, the honorable Senator from Illinois had the cordial friendship and suport of all the members of the Democratic party. Every one on this floor knows that, up to the year 1857, the honorable Senator from Illinois was looked upon with pride and confidence as one of the acknowledged leaders of the Democratic party.

Now, Mr. President, is it not a subject deserving of some inquiry; will it not naturally suggest itself to the American people to inquire how happens it that a gentleman, who for a long series of years possessed the confidence and admiration of his party, upon whom they looked with pride, whom they acknowledged as a leader, and for whom they reserved their choicest honors, should suddenly find himself separated from every Democratic State in the Union, and from the whole body of his Democratic associates here and in the other House. What magic has effected this change in the universal sentiment towards him? What occult power has been brought to bear upon the Senator from Illinois, that to-day he complains and whines that he is the subject of a common assault by gentlemen who were formally with him, and who, he says, are pursuing him with ruthless malignity? How happens it that the Senator from Illinois forgot to touch that part of the recent history of the country in his speech? I propose to commend myself to the consideration of that part of the history.

When, in 1854, the Kansas-Nebraska bill was before us—I must be guilty of some repetition; it is impossible to avoid it when a question has been worn so threadbare—there were three distinct sentiments professed upon this floor in relation to the government of the Territories of the United States. The gentlemen on the other side of the Chamber professed the principle that the Congress of the United States had the power to govern the Territories, and that there was to be found in the Constitution of the United States no prohibition against exercising that power so as to exclude slavery; and they therefore went for excluding slavery from the Territories by the power of Congress, which had an admitted power to govern them. The southern members of the Democratic party, with some of the members from the North, agreed with the Republican party that the Congress of the United States had the undoubted power to govern the Territories; but they held that there was a limitation to that power to be found in the Constitution of the United States, which limitation prevented the Congress of the United States from exercising the power to exclude slavery; but, on the contrary, imposed it as a duty upon Congress to protect property in slaves, just as all other property. The third school had at its head, at that time, the venerable Senator from Michigan, now in the Department of State. With him were joined the honorable Senator from Illinois, and the honorable Senator from Michigan then, Mr. Stuart, I think. They held that the sole power of Congress was to institute an organic act, as they termed it; that the sole power was to give, as it were, a constitution to the Territories by which the people might be brought together in organized form, and that when the people were thus brought together in an organized form, in a legislative capacity, they possessed inherent sovereignty, just as a State, and had a right to do in relation to slavery just as they pleased.

Those were the three principles advocated upon this floor. I think I state them correctly. I try to do so, at all events. When we were discussing the principle to be introduced into the Kansas-Nebraska bill, we all agreed that we were opposed to the principles advocated by the Republican party. We all agreed that whether Congress had the power or not to exclude slavery from the Territories, it was injurious to exercise that power; that Congress ought not to intervene. That is what we said, and all the Senators from the South concurred with that. When we came further to determine what was to be done, after having decided that Congress should not intervene, we split. The Democrats of the South, and some of the Democrats of the North agreeing with them, in our caucus meetings, in discussing the principles of the bill, in framing its provisions, in preparing it for discussion in the Senate, said: "The Territorial Legislature has no power to exclude the people of the South, or their property, from the Territories, because the Territories are governed by Congress as a trustee for all the States; the Territorial Legislature can get no power but the power that Congress gives it, and Congress itself has no power to exclude our property from the Territories, which belong to us as well as to the free States." The Senator from Illinois said differently. The Senator from Illinois said that he believed the Territorial Legislature had the right, whilst the people of the

Territory were in a territorial organization, to exclude slavery if they pleased. We split on that; we could not agree. I admit all that the Senator said here the other day as to it. He said so then; he says now. I complain exactly of that consistency; because when we could not agree, he said that he would agree with us to submit it to the courts, and if the courts decided in our favor, he would give up and join us; and we agreed if the courts decided against us, that we would give up and join him. It is that very consistency that is complained of; and I shall proceed to prove it.

It is bad faith when the honorable Senator no longer worships at the shrine of constitutional principle. Professing to agree to leave the matter to the decision of the courts, professing to respect the courts in their decisions, he has gone astray after false gods, and is now worshiping the idols of evasion and circumvention. Sir, I do not state of my own authority the position of the honorable Senator from Illinois, I read again from his speech the other day. He is speaking of the power of a Territorial Legislature to exclude slavery. The Senator from Illinois is right in saying that his opinion was clearly explained at the time. He asserted the power in the Territorial Legislature:

"I believe the power existed; others believed otherwise; we agreed to differ; we agreed to refer it to the judiciary; we agreed to abide by their decision; and I, true to my agreement, referred my colleague to the courts to find out whether the power existed or not. The fact that I referred him to the courts has been cited as evidence that I did not think individually that the power existed in a Territorial Legislature. After the evidences that I produced yesterday, and the debate just read upon the Trumbull amendment, no man who was an actor in those scenes has an excuse to be at a loss as to what my opinion was."

The Senator from Illinois is right; his opinion was clearly expressed at the time. He asserted the power in the Territorial Legislature:

"But it was not my opinion that was to govern; it was the opinion of the court on the question arising under a territorial law after the Territory should have passed a law upon the subject. Bear in mind that the report introducing the bill was that these questions touching the right of property in slaves were referred to the local courts, to the territorial courts with a right of appeal to the Supreme Court of the United States When that case shall arise, and the court shall pronounce its judgment, it will be binding on me, on you, sir, and on every good citizen. It must be carried out in good faith; and all the power of this Government—the Army, the Navy, and the militia—all that we have—must be exerted to carry the decision into effect in good faith, if there be resistance. Do not bring the question back here for Congress to review the decision of the court, nor for Congress to explain the decision of the court. The court is competent to construe its own decisions, and issue its own decrees to carry its decisions into effect.

"We are told that the court has already decided the question. If so, there is an end of the controversy. You agreed to abide by it; I did. If it has decided it, let the decision go into effect; there is an end of it; what are we quarrelling about? Will resolutions of the Senate give any additional authority to the decision of the Supreme Court of the United States? Does it need an endorsement by the Charleston convention to give it validity? If the decision is made, it is the law of the land, and we are all bound by it. If the decision is not made, then what right have you to pass resolutions here, prejudging the question, with a view to influencing the views of the court? If there is a dispute as to the true interpretation and meaning of the decision of the court, who can settle the true construction except the court itself, when it arises in another case? Can you determine by resolutions here what the decision of the court is, or what it ought to be, or what it will be? It belongs to that tribunal. The Constitution has wisely separated the political from the judicial department of the Government. The Constitution has wisely made the courts a co-ordinate branch of the Government; as independent of us as we are of them. Sir, you have no right to instruct that court how they shall decide this question in dispute. You have no right to define their decision for them. When that decision is made, they will issue the proper process for carrying it into effect; and the Executive is clothed with the Army, the Navy, and the militia, the whole power of the Government, to execute that decree. All I ask, therefore, of you, is non-intervention; hands off. In the language of the Georgia resolutions, let the subject be banished forever from the Halls of Congress or the political arena, and referred to the Territories, with a right of appeal to the courts; and there is an end to the controversy."

Mr. President, I have read that extract at length, that all may see the precise point at which the honorable Senator from Illinois has separated himself from his Democratic brethren and the Democratic party. I have him here now, in his speech before the Senate the other day, declaring that that was the bargain; that whenever the court made the decision he would stand by it; that he had always intended to stand by it; that it was binding on him in good faith; and that the whole power of the Government should, with his consent, be called into operation for the purpose of carrying out the decision. I shall proceed presently to show that the Senator from Illinois, not once, but again and again, since 1857, has been engaged, in conjunction with gentlemen of the Black Republican party, first in endeavoring to explain away the decision that has been made, and next that he has made the broad and open avowal in the face of the country that, if the decision is made, it shall not go into effect. That is the arraignment of the honorable Senator from Illinois. Let him not go back to 1840, or 1844, or 1848, or 1852, or 1854, when he had the party with him, nor even to 1856; but let him come down to the decision of the Supreme Court of the United States, in the spring of 1857, and let him follow me while I pursue his devious track since that day.

Early in the year 1857 the Dred Scott decision was pronounced by the Supreme Court of the United States. If my recollection serves me, the decision had not been printed when we adjourned. A number of us, I think, subscribed together to obtain a number of copies from the public printer, agreeing that he should print such a number as we believed the Senate would be willing to have printed when it reassembled; and if the Senate declined to print it when it assembled, we made ourselves responsible to him for the price. It was desired that the decision of the Supreme Court should go to the country. The dissenting opinions of the two judges, who were in the minority, had been printed. The opinion of the court was still unknown. The result of its opinion was pretty well ascertained; but in a matter of that magnitude it was deemed of the last importance to have the very language of the court, and to have it spread broadcast through the land. Now, Mr. President, we are told that this decision decides nothing of what was at issue at the time; nothing of that issue which the honorable Senator from Illinois agreed to leave to the courts. I do not know any better way of ascertaining what a court decided than to do as the honorable Senator from Illinois has advised us to do—take the court's own statement of what it decided. In reference to this Dred Scott decision, it will be observed by any gentleman who chooses to refer to the nineteenth volume of Howard's Reports, that every judge gave his opinion *seriatim;* because there were numerous questions on which all did not choose to be bound, without giving a statement of their particular views; but Mr. Chief Justice Taney delivered the opinion of the court. The rest were mere statements of particular views. "Mr. Chief Justice Taney," is the expression, "delivered the opinion of the court;" and Mr. Chief Justice Taney is said to have made a syllabus of the points which he, the organ of the court, considered to have been decided by the court.

Now, in regard to the attempt to get rid of the authority of this decision on the gronnd that the questions were not before the court, and that they were *obiter dicta*, allow me to say this: it is true that when a precise point is before a court, the judgment of the court upon that point is alone that which binds the parties; but no lawyer will contradict the assertion, that those principles which the court itself lays down as being the basis upon which it arrives at its conclusion, are decisions by the court; they are not *obiter dicta. Obiter dicta*, merely passing sayings, are such views thrown out by a judge in the course of his reasoning as have no reference to the points upon which he is deciding the case; but whenever, in order to reach a result, the court proceeds to give those reasons for that result, and in giving those reasons for arriving at the result, it lays down the principles upon which the result is reached, I say those principles are considered as decided by the court. If unnecessary to its decision, they have less weight; but if the court itself declares the principles that it lays down to be necessary to its decision, and declares that it does decide them, then I say no lawyer can fail, when that case is brought up before the court, to say the court has so decided.

I do not choose to go into that at any length, nor even to read the syllabus of the decision of the Supreme Court. But what were we divided about in the year 1854, and what was it that the honorable Senator from Illinois agreed to leave to the decision of the Supreme Court of the United States, upon a case to be brought up from the local Legislature of Kansas? It was this: has Congress the power to govern the Territories of the United States, or is that power in the Territorial Legislature? Has Congress the right to exclude slavery from the Territories, or can it delegate that right to a Territorial Legislature; or has a Territorial Legislature, in the absence of any delegation of this power by Congress, an inherent right to exclude slavery? These are the points.

When this case was brought before the Supreme Court of the United States, the question of the power of Congress arose directly—no man has ever denied that—the power of Congress to declare that a slave should be free by being carried into the Territories of the United States north of the Missouri compromise line. That, then, brought directly in question the power of Congress to exclude slavery from the Territories; its power to govern them, and the limit upon that power. What did the court say? In referring to a former decision, it says:

"Perhaps the power of governing a Territory belonging to the United States"—

Observe this language—

"which has not, BY BECOMING A STATE, acquired the means of self-government"—

Taking it for granted that every man must at once admit that it is only when it becomes a State that it has acquired the power of self-government.

"Perhaps the power of governing a Territory belonging to the United States, which has not, *by becoming a State*, acquired the means of self-government, may result, necessarily, from the facts that it is not within the jurisdiction of any particular State, and is within the power and jurisdiction of the United States. The right to govern may be the inevitable consequence of the right to acquire territory. Whichever may be the source from which the power is derived, the possession of it is unquestionable."

Mr. PUGH. What is that?

Mr. BENJAMIN. I am reading the citation from Canter's case, found in the Dred Scott decision. What did the court, in commenting on that——

Mr. PUGH. I only want to ask the Senator whether, in the Dred Scott decision, it is not quoted for the purpose of being commented upon?

Mr. BENJAMIN. I am going on to show, if the Senator will permit me, that the court adopted that in the Dred Scott case. I do not think I leave quite such an open joint as that in my argument. The court, in the Dred Scott case, go on:

"It is thus clear, from the whole opinion on this point, that the court did not mean to decide whether the power was derived from the clause in the Constitution, or was the necessary consequence of the right to acquire. They do decide that the power in Congress is unquestionable, *and in this we entirely concur*, and nothing will be found in this opinion to the contrary. The power stands firmly on the latter alternative put by the court—that is, as '*the inevitable consequence of the right to acquire territory*.'"

They entirely concurred. Is that decided in the Dred Scott case?

Mr. PUGH. If the Senator asks me, I think the sentence he emphasized is expressly excluded by the language of Judge Taney. He emphasized the first paragraph; and then Judge Taney says the power stands on the last paragraph.

Mr. BENJAMIN. Well, I will give you another chance. Let us take 19 Howard, page 445, referring to that same decision in Canter's case:

"Thus it will be seen by these quotations from the opinion, that the court, after stating the question it was about to decide in a manner too plain to be misunderstood, proceeded to decide it, and announced, as the opinion of the tribunal, that, in organizing the judicial department of the government in a Territory of the United States, Congress does not act under, and is not restricted by, the third article of the Constitution, and is not bound, in a Territory, to ordain and establish courts in which the judges hold their offices during good behavior, but may exercise the discretionary power which a State exercises in establishing its judicial department, and regulating the jurisdiction of its courts, and may authorize the Territorial government to establish, or may itself establish, courts in which the judges hold their offices for a term of years only; and may vest in them judicial power upon subjects confided to the judiciary of the United States. And in doing this, *Congress undoubtedly exercises the combined power of the General and a State Government.* It exercises the discretionary power of a State government in authorizing the establishment of a court in which the judges hold their appointments for a term of years only, and not during good behavior; and it exercises the power of the General Government in investing that court with admiralty jurisdiction, over which the General Government had exclusive jurisdiction in the Territory.

"No one, we presume, will question the correctness of that opinion; nor is there anything in conflict with it in the opinion now given."

How now?

Mr. PUGH. I do not think that helps you any.

Mr. BENJAMIN. The Congress of the United States has the discretionary power of a State in the Territories. The Congress of the United States has the undoubted power to govern the Territories, as they are called.

Mr. PUGH. The Senator surely knows that the decision does not say that. It says Congress has that power in the establishment of courts and conferring admiralty jurisdiction. That very paragraph in Canter's case was debated in the Senate four years ago between the Senator from Illinois (Mr. TRUMBULL) and the Senator from Michigan, General Cass. The court's attention was drawn to it.

Mr. BENJAMIN. The court's attention was evidently drawn to it, as the Senator says; but will the Senator tell me that the Congress of the United States has the power to exercise the discretionary power of a State in a Territory, in organizing its judiciary, without having any power to govern the Territory?

Mr. PUGH. So far as the courts of the United States are concerned, it exercises the same power within the States; for it provides for settling a controversy between two individuals by the action of the Federal Government.

Mr. BENJAMIN. Does the Senator say that the Congress of the United States has power to provide for establishing judges in the States for a term of years?

Mr. PUGH. No, sir; because the Constitution forbids that; but I say, and that is what the court means, that in clothing the territorial courts with admiralty jurisdiction, first in the establishment of the courts, and next in defining their jurisdiction, they exercise powers appertaining both to the Federal and State Governments; but as to asserting that Congress had all the powers of a State Government in a Territory, it is neither in Canter's case nor in the Dred Scott case, nor any other.

Mr. BENJAMIN. Assuredly, the Supreme Court of the United States tells us exactly where they stop. They say Congress has all the powers of a State in a Territory, except where the Constitution of the United States interferes. That, perhaps, is also disputed.

Mr. PUGH. Yes.

Mr. BENJAMIN. Very well; let me read the decision:

"As we have before said"—

speaking of this territory belonging to the United States—

"It was acquired by the General Government, as the representive and trustee of the people of the United States, and it must, therefore, be held in that character for their common and equal benefit; for it was the people of the several States, acting through their agent and representative, the Federal Government, who in fact acquired the Territory in question, and the Government holds it for their common use until it shall be associated with the other States as a member of the Union.

"But until that time arrives, it is undoubtedly necessary that some government should be established, in order to organize society, and protect the inhabitants in their persons and property; and as the people of the United States could act in this matter only through the Government which represented them, and through which they spoke and acted when the Territory was obtained, it was not only within the scope of its powers, but it was its duty, to pass such laws and establish such a government as would enable those by whose authority they acted to reap the advantages anticipated from its acquisition, and to gather there a population which would enable it to assume the position to which it was destined among the States of the Union. The power to acquire necessarily carries with it the power to preserve and apply to the purposes for which it was acquired. The form of government to be *established necessarily rested in the discretion of Congress.* It was their duty to establish the one that would be best suited for the protection and security of the citizens of the United States, and other inhabitants who might be authorized to take up their abode there, and that must always depend upon the existing condition of the Territory, as to the number and character of its inhabitants, and their situation in the Territory. In some cases a government, consisting of persons appointed by the Federal Government, would best subserve the interests of the Territory when the inhabitants were few and scattered and new to one another. In other instances it would be more advisable to *commit the powers of self-government* to the people who had settled in the Territory, as being the most competent to determine what was best for their own interests. But some form of civil authority would be absolutely necessary to organize and preserve civilized society, and prepare it to become a State; and what is the best form must always depend on the condition of the Territory at the time, and the choice of the mode must depend upon the *exercise of a discretionary power by Congress, acting within the scope of its constitutional authority, and not infringing upon the rights of person or the rights of property of the citizen who might go there to reside, or for any other lawful purpose. It was acquired by the exercise of this discretion, and it must be held and governed in like manner, until it is fitted to be a State.*"

The Congress has not only the right to govern it, but the right either to govern it by delegating persons to hold authority, or by exercising its discretion and committing to the people the right of self-government—giving to the people the right of self-government; by the action of Congress, not by inherent sovereignty—a grant to be made by Congress to the people of a Territory, of self-government through their Legislature; and yet the honorable Senator from Illinois (Mr. DOUGLAS) tells us that although the Supreme Court of the United States decided in that case (a decision by which he agreed to abide) that the

Congress of the United States have the unquestioned power to govern the Territories; and although the court decided that Congress could govern them in any way it pleased in its discretion; and although the court decided that one mode of governing them was for Congress to commit to the inhabitants there a power of self-government; when Congress has committed that power, he says that the people who got it from Congress have more right than Congress itself; and that the Territorial Legislature, which draws its legislative power from a grant by Congress, can rise higher than the powers possessed by the grantor; or, in other words, that the stream can rise above its source.

Mr. PUGH. Does the Senator say that the court meant that Congress makes a grant of the power of self-government to the people of a Territory?

Mr. BENJAMIN. Clearly.

Mr. PUGH. Where does Congress get the power of self-government? The phrase is that Congress has power of self-government over a Territory. It is a contradiction in terms.

Mr. BENJAMIN. Who says that? Here is the same idol—evasion.

Mr. PUGH. If I should respond to the Senator in equal temper, I should call his an evasion. I desire to know where he finds, in the Dred Scott case, the proposition.

Mr. BENJAMIN. The court says that Congress may, without reference to the action of the people of a Territory, govern it as it pleases in its discretion. Then the court says that Congress may, instead of that, give to the people the power of self-government.

Mr. PUGH. "Commit."

Mr. BENJAMIN. Commit to the people the power of self-government. What is there absurd in that?

Mr. PUGH. There is nothing absurd in that; but I was about to say to the Senator, if that phrase fits him, I hope he will give the explanation——

Mr. BENJAMIN. The absurdity, if any, is that of the court, not mine.

Mr. PUGH. Undoubtedly in the case of Louisiana, which the Senator from Georgia cited yesterday, that act was simply preliminary, to get possession of the country, and until you have a sufficient community it is all idle to talk about self-government; but I understand that paragraph to be that, whenever the period arrives that a community is there and Congress recognizes the community, Congress has no power of self-government to grant; it has no such power. If there is any such power it comes from some other place, and I say it does not come from Congress. Congress did not have it.

Mr. BENJAMIN. What is meant by Congress committing the power of self-government to the people?

Mr. PUGH. Acknowledging it.

Mr. BENJAMIN. *Commit* means to *acknowledge?* Very well.

Mr. PUGH. In that sense. I ask the Senator how Congress can commit a power which Congress could not by any possibility have; for it is an absurdity in terms to say that Congress has the power of self-government in the Territories?

Mr. BENJAMIN. Congress has the power of government.

Mr. PUGH. Then leave the word "self" out.

Mr. BENJAMIN. Exactly, when applied to Congress. Congress has the power of government over the Territories; but when Congress commits the power to the people to govern themselves that is a power of self-government in them. It seems to me so plain that language cannot make it plainer. I cannot pursue the discussion on that point with the Senator from Ohio.

But, sir, the Supreme Court of the United States, in relation to this power of Congress and of the Territorial Legislature, has not stopped where I have just read. It has gone further, and said:

"The powers over person and property of which we speak"—

that is, the power of confiscating the slaves of the citizens of the slaveholding States, if they go into the Territories—

"are not only granted to Congress, but are in express terms denied, and they are forbidden to exercise them. And this prohibition is not confined to the States, but the words are general, and extend to the whole territory over which the Constitution gives it power to legislate, including those portions of it remaining under territorial government, as well as that covered by States. It is a total absence of power everywhere within the dominion of the United States, and places the citizens of a Territory, so far as these rights are concerned, on the same footing with the citizens of the States, and guards them as firmly and plainly against any inroads which the General Government might attempt under the plea of implied or incidental powers, and if Congres itself cannot do this; if it is beyond the powers conferred on the Federal Government it will be admitted, we presume, that it could not authorize a territorial government to exercise them. It could confer no power on any local government established by its authority to violate the provisions of the Constitution."

Congress cannot destroy the property of a citizen in his slave in a Territory. Congress can commit to the people of a Territory the power of government —the Senator says "self-government" is absurd—then, let us say the power of government; but in so committing it, the court say they presume it will be admitted that Congress cannot authorize a territorial government to exercise the powers which Congress itself is prohibited from exercising. Again:

"And if the Constitution recognizes the right of property of the master in a slave, and makes no distinction between that description of property and other property owned by a citizen, no tribunal, acting under the authority of the United States"—

And surely the Territorial Legislature, when organized, are acting under our authority—

"no tribunal, acting under the authority of the United States, whether it be *legislative*, executive, or judicial, has a right to draw such a distinction, or deny to it the benefit of the provisions and guarantees which have been provided for the protection of private property against the encroachments of the Government."

Now, Mr. President, in that connection, let me thank the honorable Senator from Mississippi for bringing the Senator from Illinois to the point the other day. We have got him at last where we can understand him. Again and again the distinguished Senator from Mississippi called upon the Senator from Illinois to define what he meant by squatter sovereignty. He was asked when and how it is that the people of a Territory acquired the right of self-government. I have here his answer. Well might the Senator from Mississippi say that the more this subject was examined and discussed, the further we got apart. What was the answer of the Senator from Illinois? It was this. Shall I call it absurd? No, sir; senatorial courtesy will not permit it; but I state it in his own language almost. I will read his words presently. When the people of this country first go into the wilderness and find there no government whatever, and then exercise that inherent right of self-defence which drives men, under the laws that God has implanted in them, to associate together in self-defence, and organize some system of law for their own protection; then, when it would seem to the common sense of universal mankind that no one could say they were wrong in doing that—then it is that the Senator from Illinois says he repudiates and opposes their power. That is the squatter sovereignty that he objects to. But when the sovereign has come in; when the trustee of all the States has taken possession of the common fund; when it has organized a government that suits it in the exercise of its discretion; and when it has committed the administration of the affairs of the Territory, with certain limitations under the Constitution of the United States, to a Territorial Legislature—then, when the sovereign is present, then the people become invested, by some magical process, with an inherent popular sovereignty that rises superior to the author of their being. That is the position of the Senator from Illinois.

In answer to the Senator from Mississippi, he said:

"Regarding squatter sovereignty as a nick-name invented by the Senator and those with whom he acts, which I have never recognized, I must leave him to define the meaning of his own term. I have denounced squatter sovereignty where you find it setting up a government in violation of law, as you do now at Pike's Peak. I denounced it this year. Where you find an unauthorized legislature, in violation of law, setting up a government without the sanction of Congress or the Constitution—that is squatter sovereignty which I oppose. *There is the case in Dacota, where you have left a whole people without any law or territorial organization, with no mode of appeal from their squatter courts to the United States courts to correct their decisions. That is squatter sovereignty in violation of the Constitution and laws of the United States.* There is a similar government set up over a part of the State of California, and a part of the Territory of Utah, called Nevada. It has had a delegate here claiming that he represented it. I have denounced that as unlawful. If that is what the Senator referred to, I am against it. All I say is, that the people of a Territory, when they have been organized under the Constitution and laws, have legislative power over all rightful subjects of legislation consistent with the Constitution of the United States."

Now, the Supreme Court of the United States says that no tribunal, *legislative*, executive, or judicial, acting under the authority of the United States, can interfere with the right of a southern citizen to his property in the Territories. The honorable Senator from Illinois says they cannot do it *until* they are organized under the authority of the United States. Which is right? He says the people of a Territory do not get the power until they are organized under the authority of the General Government. The Supreme Court of the United States says no earthly tribunal organized under the authority of the United States can exercise that power.

Now, Mr. President, I cannot go any further into the discussion of this case, because, in view of my ulterior purposes in this argument, it is unnecessary. No sooner had that decision been made than it was attacked all over the land. It was attacked by the Republican party. The honorable Senator from New Hampshire (Mr. HALE) was not satisfied with attacking the principles of the decision. The Chief Justice, in order to come at the point to which he was directing his attention, declared that he could only reach the point by taking into consideration the history of the African race on this continent, and looking back, in a historical point of view, to the date of the adoption of the Constitution; and he proceeded to give that history. He stated that at that date certain principles were prevalent in the country, and amongst them, that these unfortunate people were considered by many as having no rights which a white man was bound to respect. The honorable Senator from New Hampshire repeated here the other day the statement that this assertion of a historical fact was one of the points *decided* by the court, in defiance, I suppose, of one thousand corrections of the statement that had been made all over the United States.

Again: the honorable Senator from New York, (Mr. SEWARD,) who is not now in his seat, and whose claims upon the gratitude and confidence of his party were so ruthlessly set aside at Chicago, undertook to get rid of the decision by denouncing the court; and Senators around me will remember how, again and again, he stood up here in the Senate and insinuated, in the face of the country, that there had been a bargain between the Chief Justice and the President of the United States. He saw what the decision was; he did not attempt to evade or avoid it. He tried to get rid of its moral power by blackening the character of its author. What says the honorable Senator from Illinois? He does not do that. He now says that his bargain was that he would abide by the decision of the court when it came up from a local court in a Territory. He is not satisfied with the decision, although given by the tribunal to which we all agreed to refer it. He says he did not agree to refer it in the Dred Scott case; he agreed to refer it when a case should arise in a territory. Here is his language:

> "Bear in mind that the report introducing the bill was, that these questions touching the right of property in slaves were referred to the local courts, to the territorial courts, with a right of appeal to the Supreme Court of the United States. When *that* case shall arise, and the court shall pronounce its judgment, it will be binding on me, on you, sir, and on every good citizen.

Mr. President, I am not satisfied with that promise; and I am not satisfied with it because the honorable Senator from Illinois, upon several memorable occasions since the year 1857, has said out of the presence of the Senate that, if the decision was made, it would not bind the people of the Territory; that the case could not be so decided as to bind the Territory; that nothing that the Supreme Court could do by decision could bind the Territory; but, by the Kansas-Nebraska bill, he had fixed the South so that the people of the Territory, in defiance of the decisions of the court, could exclude slavery from the Territory.

Here, Mr. President, let me come back to an explanation of that fact which I spoke of before, and to which I asked the attention of the Senate and the country. Here stands the explanation of the sudden change that has been wrought in the relations of the Senator from Illinois with the rest of the Democratic party. It was when, in the year 1858, the year following this decision, pressed by a canvass at home, eager to return to the Senate, he joined in canvassing the State of Illinois with the gentleman who is now the candidate of the Black Republican party for the Presidency. Pressed in different portions of the State with this very argument, that he had agreed to leave the question to the court, that the court had decided it in favor of the South, and that, therefore, under the Kansas-Nebraska bill, slavery was fixed in all the Territories of the United States; finding himself going down in Illinois in that canvass, he backed out from his promise, and directly told the people of his State that, whether it had been decided or not, and no matter what the court might decide, the Kansas-Nebraska bill had fixed the power in the people of the North to make every Territory in the Union free.

In that contest the two candidates for the Senate of the United States, in the State of Illinois, went before their people. They agreed to discuss the issues; they put questions to each other for answer; and I must say here, for I must be just to all, that I have been surprised in the examination that I made again within the last few days of this discussion between Mr. Lincoln and Mr. DOUGLAS, to find that on several points Mr. Lincoln is a far more conservative man, unless he has since changed his opinions, than I had supposed him to be. There was no doging on his part. Mr. DOUGLAS started with his questions. Here they are, with Mr. Lincoln's answers:

"Question 1. I desire to know whether Lincoln to-day stands, as he did in 1854, in favor of the unconditional repeal of the fugitive slave law?

"Answer. I do not now, nor ever did, stand in favor of the unconditional repeal of the fugitive slave law.

"Question. 2. I desire him to answer whether he stands pledged to-day, as he did in 1854, against the admission of any more slave States into the Union, even if the people want them?

"Answer. I do not now, nor ever did, stand pledged against the admission of any more slave States into the Union.

"Question 3. I want to know whether he stands pledged against the admission of a new State into the Union with such a constitution as the people of that State may see fit to make.

"Answer. I do not stand pledged against the admission of a new State into the Union with such a constitution as the people of that State may see fit to make.

"Question 4. I want to know whether he stands to-day pledged to the abolition of slavery in the District of Columbia?

"Answer. I do not stand to-day pledged to the abolition of slavery in the District of Columbia.

"Question 5. I desire him to answer whether he stands pledged to the prohibition of the slave trade between the different States?

"Answer. I do not stand pledged to the prohibition of the slave trade between the different States.

"Question 6. I desire to know whether he stands pledged to prohibit slavery in all the Territories of the United States, north as well as south of the Missouri compromise line?

"Answer. I am impliedly, if not expressedly, pledged to a belief in the *right* and *duty* of Congress to prohibit slavery in all the United States Territories.

"Question 7. I desire him to answer whether he is opposed to the acquisition of any new territory unless slavery is first prohibited therein?

"Answer. I am not generally opposed to honest acquisitions of territory; and, in any given case, I would or would not oppose such acquisition, accordingly as I might think such acquisition would or would not aggravate the slavery question among ourselves."—*Debates of Lincoln and Douglas*, p. 88.

It is impossible, Mr. President, however we may differ in opinion with the man, not to admire the perfect candor and frankness with which these answers were given: no equivocation—no evasion. The Senator from Illinois had his questions put to him in his turn. All I propose to do now is to read his answer to the second question:

"The next question propounded to me by Mr. Lincoln is, can the people of a Territory, in any lawful way, against the wishes of any citizen of the United States, exclude slavery from their limits prior to the formation of a State constitution? I answer emphatically, as Mr. Lincoln has heard me answer a hundred times from every stump in Illinois, that, in my opinion, the people of a Territory can, by lawful means, exclude slavery from their limits prior to the formation of a State constitution. Mr. Lincoln knew that I had answered that question over and over again. He heard me argue the Nebraska bill on that principle all over the State in 1854, in 1855, and in 1856, and he has no excuse for pretending to be in doubt as to my position on that question."

All that was true; but see the art; the decision had not come yet; now the decision has come; now what?

"IT MATTERS NOT WHAT WAY THE SUPREME COURT MAY HEREAFTER DECIDE AS TO THE ABSTRACT QUESTION, WHETHER SLAVERY MAY OR MAY NOT GO INTO A TERRITORY UNDER THE CONSTITUTION, THE PEOPLE HAVE THE LAWFUL MEANS TO INTRODUCE OR EXCLUDE IT AS THEY PLEASE, for the reason that slavery cannot exist a day or an hour anywhere unless it is supported by local police regulations. Those police regulations can only be established by the local Legislature; and if the people are opposed to slavery, they will elect representatives to that body who will, by unfriendly legislation, effectually prevent the introduction of it into their midst. If, on the contrary, they are for it, their legislation will favor its extension. Hence, NO MATTER

WHAT THE DECISION OF THE SUPREME COURT MAY BE ON THAT ABSTRACT QUESTION, STILL THE RIGHT OF THE PEOPLE TO MAKE A SLAVE TERRITORY OR A FREE TERRITORY IS PERFECT AND COMPLETE UNDER THE NEBRASKA BILL. I hope Mr. Lincoln deems my answer satisfactory on that point."

He told us, a few days ago, that he had agreed that that very question should be submitted to and decided by the court. He held out to us here, when we altogether advocated and supported the Kansas-Nebraska bill, that we were submitting a judicial question to the courts, and that when that question was decided, the Democratic party should be a unit on the question thus decided; but when he goes home, and is pressed in a local contest, and he sees the glittering prize of a seat in this Chamber slipping from his grasp he turns his back upon his promise; he repudiates his words; he tells his people, *as he says he has told them a hundred times before*, that, even if the court decides against them, he has, in the Kansas-Nebraska act, obtained for the free States a *perfect right* to make a free Territory of every Territory in the Union, notwithstanding the decision of the court; and yet the honorable Senator stands up here and arraigns his Democratic brethren; accuses them of breach of faith; talks to them of turning him out of the party; and triumphantly appeals to the records of 1840 to show his consistency. Now, we tell him that we will not stand upon such promises any more. Once deceived a wise man may be; twice deceived, by the same person and the same means, he is a dupe and a fool. He tells us now again, "leave it to the courts," so that he may again go home, and addressing his people, say to them: "Fellow-citizens of Illinois, I have got the South for you. I have got them so that, no matter what the decision is, you can have a free Territory, and keep their slaves out always."

Well, sir, what occurred further in that controversy? His competitor was shocked at the profligacy of the Senator. His competitor said to him—and here is the argument—"everybody knows that the Dred Scott decision has determined the principle that a citizen of the South has a right to go into the Territory, and there, under the Constitution, his property is protected, and yet you are telling the people here that their legislators, when they swear to support the Constitution, can violate that constitutional provision." Mr. Lincoln held up his hands in horror at the proposition. He was bold in the assertion of his own principles; but he told the Senator from Illinois in that discussion that what he was saying was a gross outrage on propriety, and was breaking the bargain he had made. But again, sir, he told the Senator from Illinois that he did not believe in the Dred Scott decision, because, said he, if the Dred Scott decision be true, and slavery extends in the Territories under the Constitution of the United States, then it also exists in the States—it exists in Pennsylvania as well as in Kansas.

The contest ended. On the popular vote the Senator from Illinois was beaten; but according to the division of the representative and senatorial districts of the State, he was re-elected. The popular vote upon the election of members of the Senate and Legislature was one hundred and twenty-one thousand in his favor, one hundred and twenty-five thousand in favor of the Republican candidate, and five thousand votes in favor of what he called the Danities. All the State Republican officers were elected; but there was a majority of the Legislature of Illinois elected in favor of the Senator from Illinois, and he came back here in triumph.

Last spring I was forced to leave my country from an attack of a disease in the eyes, which required attention abroad. I went to get the attention of eminent oculists abroad. For six or eight months I was debarred from reading or writing. I came back just before the opening of this Congress; and I found that during my absence the honorable Senator from Illinois had been engaged in a controversy in the public journals and magazines of the country in relation to the principles that governed the Territories of the United States, and *that he had copied in those articles the very arguments that his Republican opponent in Illinois had used against him*, and was then using against the Democratic party. (Laughter.) I have got them here. First, that it may not be said that I originated this charge, after these magazine articles were printed, and after the Senator's opponent, Mr. Lincoln, had taxed him with want of good faith under the Constitution for alleging the power of the local Legislature to adopt this unfriendly legislation, in a subsequent speech, delivered at Columbus, Ohio, in September, 1859, Mr. Lincoln said to the people:

> "Judge DOUGLAS says, if the Constitution carries slavery into the Territories, beyond the power of the people of the Territories to control it as other property, then it follows logically that every one who swears to support the Constitution of the United States must give that support to that property which it needs. And if the Constitution carries slavery into the Territories beyond the power of the people to control it as other property, then it also carries it *it were not for my excessive modesty I would say that I told that very thing to Judge* DOUG- into the States, because the Constitution is the supreme law of the land. Now, gentlemen, *If* LAS *quite a year ago. This argument is here in print, and if it were not for my modesty, as I said, I might call your attention to it. If you will read it, you will find that I not only made that argument but made it better than he has since.*"

(Laughter.)

Now, let us look at Judge DOUGLAS's argument on this subject in Harper's Magazine. The Senator from Illinois, after thus deliberately violating the agreement that he made with his brother Democrats; after flying from the result of the decision which he himself had provoked and proposed; after declaring that no matter how many decisions might be made, he could always get clear of them, because he had so fixed it in the Nebraska bill that the people of the Territory could always, in spite of the decisions, make free Territories, then proceeded, in his canvass for the Presidency, to address himself to the people of the United States through a magazine; and the next trick—I am not speaking of it in the sense of dishonor or dishonesty—the next fantastic trick of the Senator, was to dress up a magazine article with the answers of his republican opponent in Illinois brought forward as discoveries by himself, and claimed as discoveries by himself, as I shall show; and he put forth to the astonished gaze of the American republic his new theory, that the word "States," when employed in the Constitution of the United States, often means "Territories." Let us first look at this new constitutional discovery. In order that I may do the Senator no injustice I will read what, I am sure, on its being read, if I had not the book in my hand, would be supposed to be a caricature of the opinions of a public man. In speaking of the clause about the surrender of fugitives slaves, he says:

> "It will be observed that the term 'State' is used in this provision, as well as in various other parts of the Constitution, in the same sense in which it was used by Mr. Jefferson, in his plan for establishing governments for the new States in the territory ceded, and to be ceded, to the United States, and by Mr. Madison, in his proposition to confer on Congress power 'to institute temporary governments for the *new States* arising in the unappropriated lands of the United States' to designate the political communities, Territories as well as States, within the dominion of the United States."

Here it is, and he goes on to prove it, as he says; and the proof is so amusing that I will relieve this rather tedious discussion by reading it for the amusement of the Senate:

> "The word 'States' is used in the same sense in the ordinance of the 13th of July, 1787, for the government of the Territory northwest of the river Ohio, which was passed by the remnant of the Congress of the Confederation, sitting in New York, while its most eminent members were at Philadelphia, as delegates to the federal convention, aiding in the formation of the Constitution of the United States.
>
> "In this sense the word 'States' is used in the clause providing for the rendition of fugitive slaves, applicable to all political communities under the authority of the United States, including the Territories as well as the several States of the Union. Under any other construction, the right of the owner to recover his slave would be restricted to the *States* of the Union leaving the Territories a secure place of refuge for all fugitives. The same remark is applicable to the clause of the Constitution which provides that 'a person charged in any *State* with treason, felony, or other crime, who shall flee from justice, and be found in *another State*, shall, on the demand of the executive authority of the *State* from which he fled, be delivered up to be removed to the State having jurisdiction of the crime.' Unless the term State, as used in these provisions of the Constitution, shall be construed to include every distinct political community under the jurisdiction of the United States, and to apply to Territories as well as to the States of the Union, the Territories must become a sanctuary for all the fugitives from service and justice, for all the felons and criminals who shall escape from the several *States*, and seek refuge and immunity in the *Territories*.
>
> "If any other illustration were necessary to show that the political communities which we now call Territories (but which, during the whole period of the Confederation and the formation of the Constitution, were always referred to as 'States' or 'new States') are recognized as 'States' in *some* of the provisions of the Constitution, they may be found in those clauses which declare that 'no *State*' shall enter into any 'treaty, alliance, or confederation; grant letters of marque and reprisal; coin money; emit bills of credit; make anything but gold and silver coin a tender in payment of debts; pass any bill of attainder, *ex post facto* law, or law impairing the obligation of contracts, or grant any title of nobility?'

"It must be borne in mind that in each of these cases where the power is not expressly delegated to Congress, the prohibition is not imposed upon the Federal Government, but upon the *States*. There was no necessity for any such prohibition upon Congress or the Federal Government, for the reason that the omission to delegate any such powers in the Constitution was of itself a prohibition, and so declared in express terms by the tenth amendment, which declares that 'the powers not delegated to the United States by the Constitution, nor prohibited by it to the States, are reserved to the States respectively, or to the people.'

"HENCE IT WOULD CERTAINLY BE COMPETENT FOR THE STATES AND TERRITORIES TO EXERCISE THESE POWERS BUT FOR THE PROHIBITION CONTAINED IN THOSE PROVISIONS OF THE CONSTITUTION; AND INASMUCH AS THE PROHIBITION ONLY EXTENDS TO THE 'STATES,' THE PEOPLE OF THE 'TERRITORIES' ARE STILL AT LIBERTY TO ERERCISE THEM, UNLESS THE TERRITORIES ARE INCLUDED WITHIN THE TERM 'STATES,' WITHIN THE MEANING OF THESE PROVISIONS OF THE CONSTITUTION OF THE UNITED STATES!!"

[The small capitals and notes of intense admiration are mine.]

That is a constitutional argument elaborately propounded to what the honorable Senator from Georgia yesterday said was the *nonsense* of the country. Mr. President, is it not observable, does not everybody see, that the Senator from Illinois was *driven* into just that nonsense when he assumed the power of the people of a Territory to exercise what he terms squatter or popular sovereignty? If they be, indeed, sovereigns, he is right; there is no prohibition on them in the Constitution of the United States, for the prohibitions are upon States alone, and not upon territorial governments. If, therefore, they be popular sovereigns, he does not get rid of his difficulty by saying that when the Constitution talks about States it means Territories, because that is not so; but he brings himself just to that *reductio ad absurdum* which, with his peculiar perspicacity, he saw straight before him: if the Territory is sovereign, as there is no restriction upon that sovereignty in the Constitution, because the Constitution restricts only the sovereignty of the States and the Federal Government, necessarily the people of a Territory have a right to raise armies, to wage war, to emit bills of credit, to exercise all those powers that the Constitution of the United States prohibits the States from exercising. In order to get rid of this direct additional absurdity into which he was plunged, he saw no other remedy than to appeal to the *nonsense* of the public with a statement that the Constitution of the United States meant "Territories" when it said "States."

But, sir, I have said that the honorable Senator from Illinois had in this magazine taken the argument used by his Republican opponent in the senatorial canvass in Illinois and put them before the people of the country as arguments against his Democratic associates who differed with him in opinion. I have read to you what Mr. Lincoln said on that subject in his speech in September, 1859. Here is what Mr. Lincoln said in the speech delivered by him in reply to Mr. DOUGLAS, at Jonesboro', on the 15th of September, 1858:

"To this JUDGE DOUGLAS answered, that they (the people of a Territory) can lawfully exclude slavery from the Territory prior to the formation of a constitution. He goes on to tell us how it can be done. As I understand him, he holds that it can be done by the Territorial Legislature refusing to make any enactments for the protection of slavery in the Territory, and especially by adopting unfriendly legislation to it. For the sake of clearness I will state it again; that they can exclude slavery from the Territory, first, by withholding what he assumes to be an indispensable assistance to it in the way of legislation; and, secondly, by unfriendly legislation. If I rightly understand him, I wish to ask your attention for a while to his position.

"In the first place, the Supreme Court of the United States has decided that any congressional prohibition of slavery in the Territories is unconstitutional—that they have reached this proposition as a conclusion from their former proposition, that the Constitution of the United States expressly recognizes property in slaves, and from that other constitutional provision, that no person shall be deprived of property without due process of law."

Pretty straightforward propositions, one would suppose.

"Hence they reach the conclusion that, as the Constitution of the United States expressly recognizes property in slaves, and prohibits any person from being deprived of property without due process of law, to pass an act of Congress by which a man who owned a slave on one side of a line would be deprived of him if he took him on the other side, is depriving him of that property without due process of law. That I understand to be the decision of the Supreme Court. I understand also that Judge DOUGLAS adheres most firmly to that decision; and the difficulty is, how is it possible for any power to exclude slavery from the Territory unless in violation of that decision? That is the difficulty.

"In the Senate of the United States, in 1856, Judge TRUMBULL, in a speech, substantially, if not directly, put the same interrogatory to Judge DOUGLAS, as to whether the people of a Territory had the lawful power to exclude slavery prior to the formation of a constitution. Judge DOUGLAS then answered at considerable length, and his answer will be found in the Congressional Globe under the date of June 9, 1856."

I have not that answer, but I have his answer of the 2d of July, 1856, which the Senator from Georgia read yesterday, in which he says:

"My answer then was, and now is"—

Here is his senatorial answer in Congress here:

"My answer then was, and now is, that if the Constitution carries slavery there, let it go, *and no power on earth can take it away;* but if the Constitution does not carry it there, no power but the people can carry it there."

Not just what he said in Illinois. Mr. Lincoln proceeds:

"The Judge said that whether the people could exclude slavery prior to the formation of a constitution or not *was a question to be decided by the Supreme Court.* He put that proposition, as will be seen by the Congressional Globe, in a variety of forms, all running to the same thing in substance—that it was a question for the Supreme Court. I maintain that when he says, after the Supreme Court have decided the question, that the people may yet exclude slavery by any means whatever, he does virtually say that it is not a question for the Supreme Court He shifts his ground. I appeal to you whether he did not say it was a question for the Supreme Court. Has not the Supreme Court decided that question? When he now says the people *may* exclude slavery, does he not make it a question for the people? Does he not virtually shift his ground, and say that it is *not* a question for the court, but for the people? This is a very simple proposition—a very plain and naked one." * * * * * *

"Again: I will ask you my friends, if you were elected members of the Legislature what would be the first thing you would have to do before entering upon your duties? *Swear to support the Constitution of the United States.* Suppose you believe, as Judge Douglas does, that the Constitution of the United States guaranties to your neighbor the right to hold slaves in that Territory—that they are his property—how can you clear your oaths unless you give him such legislation as is necessary to enable him to enjoy that property? What do you understand by supporting the constitution of a State or of the United States? Is it not to give such constitutional helps to the rights established by that constitution as may be practically needed? Can you, if you swear to support the Constitution, and believe that the Constitution establishes a right, clear your oath without giving it support? Do you support the Constitution if, knowing or believing there is a right established under it which needs specific legislation, you withhold that legislation? Do you not violate and disregard your oath? I can conceive of nothing plainer in the world. There can be nothing in the words 'support the Constitution' if you may run counter to it by refusing support to any right established under the Constitution. And what I say here will hold with still more force against the Judge's doctrine of 'unfriendly legislation.' How could you, having sworn to support the Constitution, and believing it guarantied the right to hold slaves in the Territories, assist in legislation *intended to defeat that right?* That would be violating your own view of the Constitution. Not only so, but if you were to do so, how long would it take the courts to hold your votes unconstitutional and void? Not a moment.

"Lastly, I would ask, is not Congress itself under obligation to give legislative support to any right that is established in the United States Constitution? I repeat the question, is not Congress itself bound to give legislative support to any right that is established in the United States Constitution? A member of Congress swears to support the Constitution of the United States; and if he sees a right established by that Constitution which needs specific legislative protection, can he clear his oath without giving that protection? Let me ask you why many of us who are opposed to slavery upon principle, give our acquiescence to a fugitive slave law? Why do we hold ourselves under obligation to pass such a law, and abide it when it is passed? Because the Constitution makes provision that the owners of slaves shall have the right to reclaim them. It gives the right to reclaim slaves, and that is, as Judge DOUGLAS says, a barren right, unless there is legislation that will enforce it."

Now, sir, let it not be said that I am reading Republican doctrines here, because these very passages from the speeches of Mr. Lincoln were introduced as discoveries by the Senator from Illinois—these and the other passages in relation to the confusion between a State and a Territory. When the Attorney General had replied to the magazine article of the Senator from Illinois, a rejoinder was issued, called "the rejoinder of Judge Douglas to Judge Black," in which he says, speaking of the magazine article:

"In that article, without assailing any one"—

He never assails any one—

"In that article, without assailing any one, or inpugning any man's motives, I demonstrated beyond the possibility of cavil or dispute by any fair-minded man, that if the proposition were true, as contended by Mr. Buchanan, that slavery exists in the Territories by virtue of the Constitution, the conclusion is inevitable and irresistible, that it is the imperative duty of Congress to pass all laws necessary for its protection; that there is and can be no exception to the rule that a right guarantied by the Constitution must be protected by law in all cases where legislation is essential to its enjoyment; that all who conscientiously believe that slavery exists in the Territories"—

Senators, listen to me now. The Senator from Illinois stood here last week, hour after hour, and asked what was this new issue which we were trying to force on the party, and whence its necessity. Why not stand, said he, on the platform of 1856; why not take that Cincinnati platform which we agreed to in 1856? Who is it, he says, that is forcing these new issues on the party? I have tracked him through Illinois. What did he say in his defence of the Harper's Magazine article about the necessity of putting this very resolution in the platform? He says he has demonstrated—

"That all who conscientiously believe that slavery exists in the Territories by virtue of the Constitution are bound by their consciences and their oaths of fidelity to the Constitution to support a congressional slave code for the Territories."

I deny that; but I want to show his view of what our duty is:

"And that no consideration of political expediency can relieve an honest man, who so believes, from the faithful and prompt performance of this imperative duty."

That is Judge DOUGLAS's view of our position; and yet, hour after hour, he stands up here and attacks us for doing that which he says our oaths and our consciences impose upon us, as a duty so imperative that it is impossible for us, as honest men, to avoid doing it. He says further, in the same "rejoinder:"

"I also demonstrated, in the same paper, that the Constitution, being uniform throughout the United States, is the same in the States as in the Territories—is the same in Pennsylvania as in Kansas; and, consequently, if slavery exists in Kansas by virtue of the Constitution of the United States, it must of necessity exist in Pennsylvania by virtue of the same instrument; and if it be the duty of the Federal Government to force the people of the Territory to sustain the institution of slavery, whether they want it or not, merely because it exists there by virtue of the Constitution, it becomes the duty of the Federal Government to do the same thing in all the States for the same reason.

"This exposition of the question produced consternation and dismay in the camp of my assailants."

He just copied the arguments from Mr. Lincoln's dispute with him, put them into the Harper's Magazine article, and tells us that this exposition of *his* of the constitutional rights and duties of the States of this Union produced consternation and dismay amongst his assailants! Why, Mr. President, what is there in this argument which the honorable Senator from Illinois has copied from those Republicans who again and again have attacked the decisions of the Supreme Court of the United States—that under the doctrine of the Dred Scott decision slavery exists as well in the States as in the Territories; a sophism so bald, a proposition so destitute of a shadow of foundation, that it never was used by any man who believed it, but was put forth to deceive those who could not understand the question.

What is the decision of the Supreme Court of the United States? It is this, plainly and simply: Congress has jurisdiction over and power to govern the Territories; the powers of Congress under the Constitution are limited; amongst the limitations is a prohibition to destroy and impair or confiscate the property of citizens without due process of law. Slaves are property, and therefore Congress has no power to confiscate them, to destroy them, or to impair the right of property in them, without due process of law. That is what the Supreme Court says. What has that to do with a State? Does Congress legislate for a State? Does Congress govern a State? Is there anything in the Constitution of the United States prohibiting a State from doing as it pleases in its own legislation, except a certain clause in which the prohibitions are plainly stated, and which does not include the slavery question at all. There are certain prohibitions on the States in the Constitution, and amongst them are emitting bills of credit, raising armies and navies, levying taxes or duties on imports, on exports—all these are prohibited to the States. The States are not prohibited from legislating on slavery in their own limits; but the Supreme Court of the United States hold that Congress is prohibited by the Constitution from doing so in the Territories, and yet the Senator from Illinois repeats this absurd position, that because Congress cannot destroy property in slaves in a Territory therefore State constitutions cannot destroy it in the States!

It was, Mr. President, well known to the Senator from Illinois when he penned this article, that there was nothing in it whatever. He was driven to it. Every time he discusses the question, if he holds to the principles he has promulgated in the Senate, and now adheres to before the nation, he will be driven step by step, back and back, to the Black Republican camp. Let him beware. Let him beware of the first step outside of the intrenchments of the

Constitution. Let him beware lest he gets so far that return becomes impossible. He has already got to using their arguments, to adopting their principles, and after vaunting here that he is the embodiment of the Democratic party, and offering indulgence and quarter to all Democratic Senators and all Democratic States that disagree with him, he joins in the cry that Democratic sentiments, truly expounded, lead to disunion.

Sir, I have trespassed on the attention of the Senate rather longer than I intended. I shall be as brief as possible for the remainder of the time I shall occupy. The Senator from Illinois, the other day, went further. He has not only evaded, avoided, and circumvented the South by the Nebraska bill, if, indeed, it be susceptible of the construction he gives it, and confers on the people of the Territories the right he now alleges, but, with all his promises, the cloven foot again sticks out. He warns us—yes, Senators, he warns us—that if the Tennessee resolution is adopted at Baltimore he will explain away that, too. Nothing can bind him, according to his present statements. Let me read this Tennessee resolution, and I will ask every man within the sound of my voice whether it does not seem to be as plain and clear as the English language can make it? Pass it, and he tells you, it will not bind him. He says it has a double construction and a double meaning. He has prepared everybody for a double meaning to it. He asked the Senator from Ohio to read it; and here it is.

"Mr. Pugh read, as follow:

"*Resolved*, That all citizens of the United States have an equal right to settle with their property in the Territories, and that under the decision of the Supreme Court, which we recognize as an exposition of the Constitution, neither their rights of person or property can be destroyed or impaired by congressional or territorial legislation."

I confess that I read it over and over, and could not see a loop to hang a doubt on. All the citizens of the United States have an equal right to settle with their property in the Territories, and no territorial legislation can impair it. That is the Tennessee resolution. What is the warning given to us by the Senator from Illinois. Here it is:

"We have had predictions that the party was to be reunited by the adoption of that resolution. The only objection that I have to it is, that it is liable to two constructions."

The Cincinnati platform that he warns us to stick to—that, of course, is not Oh, no? But this will be liable to two constructions, and I have puzzled my brain for an hour to get at that other construction. I will read what the Senator said, and perhaps other Senators may be more fortunate than I have been. I think I have got a glimpse. He says it is liable to two constructions—

"And certainly and inevitably will receive two, directly the opposite to each other, and each will be maintained with equal pertinacity."

We know what the South will maintain under that resolution; and who will maintain any other construction? Surely, the Senator from Illinois means that he will, because he knows we will not. We can see but one meaning, and no man imbued with constitutional principles can discover but one, and that is, that all citizens—those who own slaves, as well as those who own horses—have a right to go with their property into the Territories—have an equal right to go there; and that their property shall not be impaired. But the Senator from Illinois says there is another construction that will be maintained, and persistently maintained. And what is it? He says:

"The resolution contains, in my opinion, two truisms; and fairly considered, no man can question them."

What is the fair consideration he gives it?

"They are, first, that every citizen"—

Not "all the citizens." The resolution says all the citizens. He says every citizen. But I will show you why he says so:

"Every citizen of the United States has an equal right in the Territories: that whatever right the citizen of one State has may be enjoyed by the citizens of all the States."

See how he is changing it now!

"That whatever property the citizen of one State may carry there, the citizens of all the States may carry."

And then they will go on with the old Republican objection, that we are all at perfect liberty to go into the Territories without our property; that we are all on an equal footing. The old Republican argument that was brought up here in the discussions on the Kansas-Nebraska bill in 1854, the Senator from Illinois tenders to us now for the canvass of 1860. He will tell us, "You are not excluded from the Territory; a northern man goes with his horses, you may go with horses; a northern man goes with a cow, you may go with a cow; a northern man does not go with a slave, and you shall not go with a slave;" and that is the equality that he says it means. The Senator from Illinois is kind in warning us in advance this time how this proposition will be got rid of. The South will be fools if they do not take advantage of the warning, and see if something cannot be devised which the astute and practiced ingenuity of the Senator from Illinois cannot get around, if the English language can hold him. Now he says:

"And on whatever terms the citizens of one State can hold it, and have it protected, the citizens of all States can hold it and have it protected, without deciding what the right is which still remains for decision."

So that the Tennessee platform will leave us just where we are now. What is his objection to it?

"I want no double dealing, or double construction."

That is his objection. He wants things clear, plain, and straight; and then when we ask that they shall be put down clear, plain, and straight, he abuses us for making new tests in the party; talks about assaults on him; kept the Senate occupied for eight mortal hours, whilst he was attacking every man and every State in the entire Union that would not support his pretensions for the Presidency.

Now, Mr. President, the people have at last come to this point; the Democratic delegates of the South have come to this point. I speak not of the delegates in either House of Congress. It is the fashion to speak of congressional dictation, in a certain class of public journals under the control of certain public men, and yet one would suppose that a seat in Congress affords at least some *prima facie* probability of the possession of the confidence of the constituency, and that the unanimous concurrence of opinion of the chosen representatives of the Democracy, both of States and constituencies, is some *prima facie* proof of what Democratic principles are. But all that is nothing. In modern slang, this is a Yancey and caucus platform, and we are congressional dictators. I, therefore, leaving out of view the opinions of members of Congress in both branches of the General Assembly of the United States, now say that it has been demonstrated by the delegates of the South, sent by the State conventions from primary meetings, that the time has come when all constitutional rights guarantied to us under the decision of the Supreme Court—which was taken by the Senator from Illinois and his coadjutors as the common arbiter of our dispute—shall be acknowledged; that all that we demand shall be put down in the bond; that there shall be no longer a doubt in relation to it.

Mr. President, when mere private rights of property are concerned, when the question is, who owns a farm, or who owns a horse, or who is entitled to $100, it is an old aphorism of the law, *misera est servitus, ubi jus aut vagum aut incertum est*—wretched and deplorable is the slavery where the law which governs a man's right is vague or uncertain. And shall we, we who represent Democratic States and Democratic constituencies, be asked why it is that we will not leave these rights, on which they rest for their property, which are even vital to their existence, open to doubt and denial? Shall we be asked why it is that we demand that the charter of these rights be written clearly, plainly, beyond the possibility of doubt or misconstruction? Oh, no, says the Senator from Illinois, "in 1856 we were unanimous upon the Cincinnati platform; I have given it a construction, and the Charleston convention has backed my construction, and I am the Democratic party;" and it is his construction, and the construction adopted by a minority at Charleston, that he presents to us here, and asks us by what right we call for something plainer or clearer as the charter of our constitutional privileges? Miserable and deplorable is the slavery where the law governing the property of the individual is doubtful or uncertain. Degrading and dishonoring to a State is it when its sovereignty cannot ask for an expression or acknowledgment of its sovereign rights in an assembly of equals. The people of the South do not mean to be put off this time with any doubtful or vague construction. The Senator from Illinois is opposed to double meanings and double constructions; he dislikes the Tennessee platform on that ground. We share his dislike; *fas est ab hoste doceri*—we will be taught by him. We will ask that everything in our platform be put down plainly and clearly.

Mr. President, the honorable Senator from Illinois, in the plentitude of his power, tells us that the Democratic platform has been adopted, and backs him. He next tells us that it is glory enough for him to have been supported by a majority of the delegates of the Democratic party at a convention; and then with an allusion, somewhat transparent, to a course of proceeding by others which would be agreeable to him, he says that when others got a majority he sent word to his friends to vote for them. He does not say that he thinks everybody ought to send word to vote for him, but he leaves it to us, if we are generous or liberal, to draw our own conclusions. Now, Mr. President, I know what happened at that convention only from the public records of the country, and the report of its delegates. It is reported that, as his highest vote, upon one or two ballots, the honorable Senator from Illinois received one hundred and fifty-two and a half votes, and I think that was the highest.

Mr. PUGH. For several ballots—seven or eight.

Mr. BENJAMIN. How did he get them? Were there one hundred and fifty-two delegates in the convention of whom he was the choice?

Mr. PUGH. Certainly; they expressed it by their vote.

Mr. BENJAMIN. Oh, that was part of the arrangement by which those who were not candidates for the Presidency were caught, but the truth of history will leak out in despite of those little arrangements. (Laughter.) I had here amongst my papers, I think, the speech of a delegate, who explains this majority.

Mr. PUGH. State the substance of it. If it was said at Charleston I shall recollect it.

Mr. BENJAMIN. Well, sir, I will state the substance of it; I cannot find the extract I had, and I shall have to affix it to my speech. Gentlemen have doubtless seen it. Scarcely had the Charleston convention met, and a committee been appointed on organization, when it reported an organization of presidents, vice presidents, and secretaries, and sprung this resolution on the convention *instanter*—the convention had previously adopted the rules of the previous Democratic conventions—

"The committee further recommend"—

The subject was not committed to them at all—

"The committee further recommend that the rules and regulations adopted by the Democratic conventions of 1852 and 1856 be adopted by this convention for its government; with this additional rule:

"That any State which has not provided or directed by its State convention how its votes may be given, the convention will recognize the right of each delegate to cast his individual vote."

As a certain gentleman was a candidate for the Presidency—Heaven preserve the country from candidates for the Presidency!—wherever the gentleman's friends were in the majority, they had taken special pains, by preorganization, to get a resolution passed at the State conventions instructing the delegates to vote as a unit, and thus they fastened down every man in a minority in the United States, and in spite of himself got his vote cast for the Senator from Illinois, although he was opposed to him. But the conventions in other States leaving the Democratic delegates to the instincts of their own judgment; leaving in operation the time-honored traditions of the party; not tying up their delegations by instructions, left them to act as they might think proper; and when they got to Charleston, by forcing the votes of all the minorities that were against Mr. DOUGLAS, and freeing the hands of all the minorities that were in his favor, his friends had cast for him all the minorities, both those for him and those against him, in all the United States. That is the way he got one vote more than half the convention. Now, what I was looking for was this: the distinct statement of a delegate from Massachusetts, (Mr. BUTLER,) that there were fifteen steady, persistent votes against the Senator from Illinois from the State of New York alone. I am telling you what Mr. Butler said.

Mr. PUGH. I read his speech last night; I think he said twelve.

Mr. BENJAMIN. I read it this morning; it said fifteen. It may have changed since last night.

Mr. PUGH. Very well; fifteen delegates.

Mr. BENJAMIN. He says there were fifteen delegates from New York alone who were steady, persistent opponents of Mr. DOUGLAS; yet those votes were cast for him. There was a minority in Indiana; but those votes were cast for him. There were minorities in other States, which I added up; and instead of having a majority of the delegates of the Democratic party throughout the United States in his favor, Mr. DOUGLAS was in a lean minority of but one-third of the delegates, and that one-third exclusively from Republican States. The whole Democratic party of the United States, as its Democratic electoral votes will testify, was opposed to him unanimously. Mr. Butler says so. My friend from Minnesota (Mr. RICE) has just handed me the extract in the Constitution of this morning; and I will read not the whole of it, but portions of it, and if I am wrong in my memory as to fifteen, I will give up.

Mr. PUGH. I read it in the Herald last night.

Mr. BENJAMIN. Mr. Butler, in giving an account to his constituents at a meeting called to censure him, but which approved and endorsed him after he was through, said:

"In New York there were fifteen votes opposed to Judge DOUGLAS from first to last, yet her thirty-five votes were cast for him on every ballot; in Ohio, six votes"

Mr. PUGH. Not one.

Mr. BENJAMIN—

"In Indiana, five votes; In Minnesota, two votes opposed to him, yet by that rule cast for him, so that the majority was more apparent than real."

I leave out the six votes from Ohio. The Senator from Ohio, who was a delegate himself, must certainly know better than the delegate from Massachusetts, and I abandon the point to his superior knowledge; but here, without counting any more, fifteen in New York, five in Indiana, two in Minnesota, make twenty-two. Take twenty-two from one hundred and fifty-two, and there remain one hundred and thirty, without counting a solitary vote against him from the State of Ohio. But, sir, I will not enter into these minutiæ, which ought not to be entered into in the Senate, and which I certainly never would have thought of speaking of, but for the constant vaunt of the Senator from Illinois that the majority was his, and he was entitled to a nomination; that the party had backed his principles, and that we were all rebels against his high majesty. I should not have inquired into this matter but for that. And now what does this delegate say as the sum total of what occurred? He says:

"Now, with the South opposed to Judge DOUGLAS, even to a disruption of the party; with every Democratic free State voting against him; with two-thirds of the delegation of the great State of Pennsylvania firmly against him, one-half nearly of New York hostile, New Jersey divided, and the only State in New England where the Democracy can have much hope (Connecticut) nearly equally balanced, what was it the part of wisdom for your delegate to do?"

That is the question Mr. Butler presents to his constituency. What does he say?

"I found also that Judge DOUGLAS was in opposition to almost the entire Democratic majority of the Senate of the United States. No matter who is right or who is wrong, it is not a pleasant position for a candidate of the Democratic party."

This is Mr. Butler's language:

"I found him opposed by a very large majority of the Democratic members of the House of Representatives."

We have watched him here:

"It is doubtless all wrong that this should be so, yet so it is. I have heard that the sweetest wine makes the sourest vinegar, but I never heard of vinegar sour enough to made sweet wine. Cold apathy and violent opposition are not the prolific parent of votes. I found, worse than all for a Democratic candidate for the Presidency, that the Clerk of the Republican House of Representatives was openly quoted as saying that the influential paper controlled by him would either support DOUGLAS or SEWARD, thus making himself, apparently, an unpleasant connecting link between them.

"With these facts before me, and impressing upon me the conviction that the nomination of Judge DOUGLAS could not be made with any hope of safety to the Democratic party, what was I to do? I will tell you what I did do, and I am afraid it is not what I ought to have done. Yielding to your preference, I voted seven times for Judge DOUGLAS, although my judgment told me that my votes were worse than useless, as they gave him an appearance of strength in the convention which I felt he had not, in fact, in the Democratic party."

That is the gentleman who stands up here, and as the embodiment of the Democratic party challenges the entire body of his Democratic fellow-Senators.

Now, Mr. President, all that I have said has been said somewhat in indignation. It was not in human nature not to feel indignation at the charges so profusely scattered against me and my friends, and my State; but still, sir, after all "more in sorrow than in anger." Up to the years 1857 and 1858, no man in this nation had a higher or more exalted opinion of the character, the services, and the political integrity of the Senator from Illinois than I had. I can appeal to those who may have heard me in the last presidential canvass, in my State, where, for months together, day and night, I was travelling in support of the Democratic party, and helping as far as my humble abilities would admit, to break down the Know-Nothing party, which had then a decided majority of the voters of our State inscribed in its lodges. We succeeded in that contest. The canvass was a successful one; and it did so happen that, in the course of that canvass, I had again and again to appeal to my Democratic fellow-citizens of the State of Louisiana to stand by the gallant Democracy of the North who stood by us, to frown down this new organization, whose only effect could be to injure the Democratic candidate and his success; and then, in speaking of that bright galaxy of Democratic talent, Democratic integrity, and Democratic statesmanship, that I now see gathered and clustered around me, the central figure was the honored portrait of the Senator from Illinois.

Sir, it has been with reluctance and sorrow that I have been obliged to pluck down my idol from his place on high, and refuse to him any more support or confidence as a member of the party. I have done so, I trust, upon no light or unworthy ground. I have not done so alone. The causes that have operated on me have operated on the Democratic party of the United States, and have operated an effect which the whole future life of the Senator will be utterly unable to obliterate. It is impossible that confidence thus lost can be restored. On what ground has that confidence been forfeited, and why is it that we now refuse him our support and fellowship? I have stated our reason to-day. I have appealed to the record. I have not followed him back in the false issue or the feigned traverse that he makes in relation to matters that are not now in contest between him and the Democratic party. The question is not what we all said or believed in 1840 or in 1856. How idle was it to search ancient precedents, and accumulate old quotations from what Senators may have at different times said in relation to their principles and views. The precise point, the direct arraignment, the plain and explicit allegation made against the Senator from Illinois is not touched by him in all of his speech.

We accuse him for this, to wit: that having bargained with us upon a point upon which we were at issue, that it should be considered a judicial point; that he would abide the decision; that he would act under the decision, and consider it a doctrine of the party; that having said that to us here in the Senate, he went home, and under the stress of a local election, his knees gave way; his whole person trembled. His adversary stood upon principle and was beaten; and lo! he is the candidate of a mighty party for the Presidency of the United States. The Senator from Illinois faltered. He got the prize for which he faltered; but lo! the grand prize of his ambition to-day slips from his grasp because of his faltering in his former contest, and his success in the canvass for the Senate, purchased for an ignoble price, has cost him the loss of the Presidency of the United States.

Here were two men, struggling before the people of a State on two great sides of a political controversy that was dividing the Union, each for empire at home. One stood on principle—was defeated. To-day, where stands he? The other faltered—received the prize; but, to-day, where stands he? Not at the head of the Democratic party of these United States. He is a fallen star. We have separated from him. He is right in saying we have separated from him. We have separated from him, not because he held principles in 1856 different from ours. We have separated from him, not because we are intolerant of opposition from anybody, for the Senator from Ohio (Mr. PUGH) is an honored member of our organization. We separated from him because he has denied the bargain that he made when he went home; because, after telling us here in the Senate that he was willing that this whole matter should be decided by the Supreme Court, in the face of his people, he told them that he had got us by the bill; and that, whether the decision was for us or against us, the practical effect was to be against us; and because he shows us now again that he is ready to make use of Black Republican arguments used against himself at home, and to put them forth against the Democratic party in speeches here in the Senate.

Now, Mr. President, this will be represented as an attack on the honorable Senator from Illinois; but I finish my speech, as he did his, by saying "the Senate will bear me witness that I have not spoken on this subject until attacked; all I have said is in self-defence I attack no man, and the world shall know if ever I speak again, it shall be in self-defence." (Laughter.) Mr. President, the best defence is to carry the war into the enemy's country. I belong to no school of politicians that stand on the defensive. If attacked, I strike back, and ever shall. If the Senator from Illinois wants the world to know that he spoke only in self-defence, let the same measure of justice be meted out to me, and in answer to any one who can, by possibility, consider what I have said as an attack, I reply "self-defence." (Laughter.) I wish my speech qualified just like that of the honorable Senator from Illinois. If his is an attack, mine is; if his is "self-defence" against some unknown person, mine also is "self-defence" against some body that has attacked me and my State, whose name I do not know. (Laughter.) That is just my position, I state it plainly; I am sorry the Senator is not here to hear it stated.

www.ingramcontent.com/pod-product-compliance
Lightning Source LLC
LaVergne TN
LVHW011143110826
845150LV00008B/2491
* 9 7 8 1 4 1 8 1 9 2 0 4 4 *